She

Wears

Pain

Like

Diamonds

Alfa

Bestselling author of
I Find You in the Darkness

CASTLE POINT BOOKS
NEW YORK

Introduction

You watch entranced as she races through her days, *just like you do,* but she is unstoppable with seemingly endless energy. Oh, and she smiles a lot. The kind that shows the indentations on both sides of perfectly painted lips. *And you wish you could smile just as easily.* Surely, she has never experienced the severity of pain that causes faces to sour.

How does she do it? How does she maintain control during life's uncontrollable trials?

The reality is *we don't see her* when she finds her quiet place and lets her shoulders fall. We don't see her scrub her face and find herself unrecognizable in the mirror. We don't see her in the moments that she lays her sword down and lets the past envelop her. We don't see her fall apart. *But she does.* She is more like you than you realize. But tomorrow she will rise and lift her weighted shoulders, and she will smile for the life she is grateful for.

This book is dedicated to
the beautiful souls who carry on exquisitely
in spite of invisible illnesses, autoimmune
disorders, and mental health challenges.
I am in awe of your strength.

You are the strongest souls I know.

Everyone becomes a poet
when their heart is screaming.

—A l f a

Contents

RIGHT NOW,

IN THE MIDDLE OF DESPAIR,

DIAMONDS ARE BEING BIRTHED

IN THE EARTH'S MANTLE.

MANTLE

Brittle

Can she let you *into* the broken parts?

The crevices unseen by a naked eye,

The brittle parts that are held together with
strands of determination and defiance that
shimmer like diamonds,

The place that shows her brimstone past
and its hell-fire damnation?

The brittle parts she is most ashamed of:

Can she let you in?

Eradicate Normalcy

Aren't we more than the masks we wear
for our peers? We smile, we shake our heads
in agreement. We show up at family functions
because it is expected of us.

A birthday party for our bloodline.

A holiday we cannot let pass.

We do it because we always have, and we
cannot think of one excuse befitting
our absence.

But if truth be known, we would skip it all.
Eradicate normalcy. We would discard the
mandatory, the days that are already planned
out for us before we even jot them down in
our calendars.

Going with the Flow

She is learning.

She has acquired the knack

for dressing up

or down

for any occasion.

Planes Shifting

When love and pain dance within the lining of our souls, they build for us a defense system while our insides are being reformed and repaired.

We feel our planes shifting and colliding with each other as we continue to navigate a world that graciously fills our reservoirs every time we are on the edge of depletion.

Carrying Memories

We carry the memories, the painful
experiences that our minds refuse to let go.
We have accepted them because we had no
choice. We have absorbed them into the
linings of our hearts, but we carry them.

We package them in pretty purses and wear
them over our shoulders with pride. We carry
them and rock them on our daily catwalk.

Wishes

She has told them countless times

and in countless ways.

She watches as their promises blow

like dandelions

across the vacancy

they've yet to fill.

She has told them.

She is empty.

But her wishes

are still just broken promises.

Gut Wisdom

When they tell you that you're over-sensitive,

but your gut is in knots, believe your gut.

It always has your back.

The people who want to downplay your hurt

do not.

Sandwiched

She always feels stuck in the middle,

sandwiched between other lives,

a condiment to enhance their existence.

And she wonders if her life will ever truly

be her own.

Taken Care Of

She takes care of them, but she so badly
wants to be *taken care of*. And that makes
her feel selfish and weak all at once because
she was raised to never depend on anyone and
to handle every facet of her life herself.

But every once in a while, the tiredness
overtakes her, and she is overcome with
loneliness and a need to be taken care of.

Flicker

You can have an inferno in your heart,

but if you do not feed it,

it will barely flicker.

Your Epitaph

Just because a person made you

their personal conquest,

and made you submit

to the evil of this world,

does not mean

that you will wear

your past as your epitaph.

Graceful

Grace is the way

she handles those

who would douse her in shame

and light the match.

Fear Flies

When you open the closets

and set the screams free,

fear flies away.

Monumental Possibilities

We have the makings

of monuments in our souls.

Towers that can only be fashioned by

our own individual and unique talents.

Imagine the legacy each person is capable

of leaving behind for generations to behold.

Alabaster Intentions

She cried crimson

and prayed in alabaster hues.

A reflection of good

overcoming evil.

Undefined Boundaries

Love has no boundaries.

Time and space cannot diminish

what the Universe has implanted.

Because even though they are apart,

he will always be *a part* of her.

Love in Limbo

In times of reflection,

she feels the numbness coming back,

the bittersweet paralysis

that is a side effect

of loving him.

In Tune

When the tune of their past plays, it finds
her and serenades her with a love song she
has never been able to get out of her head.

Trussed Up

Her heart was always afraid to stay,

but even more frightened to leave.

She ran in circles trying to untie
their connection,

only to get more trussed up.

Pursuit of Peace

She fought so hard over the years.

For him. For them. For herself.

Her heart was always on alert and her battle gear at the front door.

She never knew when she would get the call that she had to go.

And all she wanted was the peace that she fought so valiantly for.

Questions and Answers

It's funny.

The beginning of a relationship,
as you woo each other,
is freely asking questions and providing
answers at the drop of a hat.

The ending is asking questions that have
no chance of ever being answered.

Dragging Hearts

She has met them

in every shape

and form—

Hearts that never

asked to be dragged

across landscapes

they never wanted

to visit.

Being Transparent

You have scars

and you have tried

to hide them because

you think they will

frighten anyone who

tries to love you.

But the person

who is meant to love you

will look at those scars

and promise to never

add more.

Forces

She held it all inside,

tipping the scales

with her heavy mental load.

She held it in

and battled the forces

wreaking hell.

She held it in to maintain

peace in her home.

Protecting Your Soul

They branded her crazy

when she walked away from toxicity.

They called her weak

when she refused to battle with narcissism.

They labeled her unfeeling

when she closed her eyes to the pain.

But the boundaries were set,

and it was time to ensure

protection for her soul.

Light Step

She treads with a light step

to prevent her heavy heart

from breaking in two.

Open the Windows

Her regret has been shaped

by people and moments

she can never get back.

It is time to open

the windows of her soul,

and release them all.

This is the only chance she has

to make room for hope.

Attune Your Ears

Attune your ears

to what the world is really saying,

not what you hope it is saying.

Sometimes silence says it all.

You have to be prepared to listen.

Enforcing Respect

We set an example in how we maintain
relationships by every barrier we erect,
and by how often we allow visitors inside
our personal spaces.

Cosmos

If you wonder how she acquired

that confidence you are so envious of,

you only have to trek the stars

she leaves in her wake.

She has battled the cosmos to get

where she is today,

and that makes

a woman fearless

and her step powerful.

Moving Mountains

Moving mountains requires persistence
and pressure. So instead of succumbing
to disasters that rocked her world,
she dug until she unearthed diamonds.
She wears them proudly as a reminder
that when your life erupts, it is making way
for a beautiful and fertile landscape.

Ribbons

And even though she has moved on,

she still finds ribbons of herself left behind.

They're scattered across the horizon,

dappling the ground like birthday confetti.

So she scoops as she journeys, and hopes that

she has gathered the most important keepsakes.

Mind Dropping

Just because my mind

had to drop you in the past

doesn't mean my heart

won't carry you

into the future.

Trying to Breathe

There are days when I avoid anything
that breathes.

Because on those days it is taking
everything I have to inhale and exhale.

Blazes

Her eyes are veiled and her smile

is painted on thick.

You have no way of knowing

the inferno that rages inside,

and how meticulously it burns

every board of every bridge she crossed

to get to today.

Raw Strength

Raw strength can be defined

as the innermost power

that is only discovered

when your body

and mind

are severed

in two.

Expectations of Envy

You will never live up to their expectations
if they are not your expectations.
If you do not achieve success with your whole
heart invested, your path is never truly
your own.

Two

I count them by twos:

Arms that push away,

ears that do not listen,

eyes that avert my presence,

lips that lie

and still beg

to be kissed.

Enough

He begs for my forgiveness

and says he wants to try again,

but he cannot answer

the question of why

I was not enough for him

the first go around.

The Shine Wears Off

You will try again. You will mistake the renewed infatuation with true and everlasting love.

Then the shine will rub off, and chances are, it will all go back to the way it was before you broke up.

A person doesn't have the right to break you and come back at their will; *not unless you allow them to.*

If you keep letting them hurt you, then you are setting the pattern for the relationship.

You are enough.

You deserve someone who sees you as more than enough.

Attractive Traits

Do not compare your life to a status or a selfie. You are only viewing a fraction of a second of a person's real life. You're focusing on a highlight reel that we are all guilty of displaying on occasion.

The truth is, that person's life is much like your own. Filled with stresses and challenges.

Be you. Be authentic.

Transparency is one of the most attractive traits in a person.

Sight Unseen

If the only thing that matters to you are looks that qualify as arm candy, then you cannot say that true love is your number one priority.

If it's real and meaningful love you crave, then you might find it in the most unexpected of places and from the most unexpected of people.

If your heart is open, it has its own vision.

It is seeking a soul connection.

I often wonder if it would be easier to find true love if we met the inner person before we fell for the outward appearance.

For Eternity

It is not possible

to douse

the flame

in a heart

that burns

in love

for eternity.

Help Them Up

Success is unfulfilling if you squash everyone on your way up.

Helping others with the same dream does not stop you from achieving success.

They Like the Acquisition

Why don't they stay?

They like the acquisition.

They work hard to make

you fall, and they deserve

an Emmy for their role

as your savior.

They like to pursue,

but once they have

conquered your defenses,

the appeal ends.

They like the acquisition,

but not the responsibility

that comes with love.

Glowing

Oh, how differently she glows

when her heart is full of

sunshine instead of clouds.

The more she shines,

the more she attracts

the warmth she has

always craved.

Leveled

She has been leveled.

Shot down by a world that views her as

the enemy.

Her intelligence has been assaulted.

Her heart bound and imprisoned.

Made to dance like a puppet

for the amusement of those

who laughed openly at her confinement.

She has been forced to crawl through

trenches seeking freedom.

She has been leveled.

But she clawed her way out

and up.

So when she meets you at

eye level, and doesn't flinch,

pay her the respect she deserves.

Guests

If she is honest,

she still has the hopes stored.

Sometimes she lets them out,

and lets them roam the halls

of the house they built together.

She lets them *go back home*,

the way her heart

sometimes wishes it could.

Secrecy

Be careful to whom you reveal

your innermost secrets.

Some people are not capable

of handling your heart

in the raw.

Be wary of those who clamor

for your transparency,

but judge your scars.

A Letter to My Heart

I am sorry for *not being there* for you.

I am sorry for *ignoring your cries*.

For not thinking things through before I threw you out to the most eager attention-giver on the block. I am sorry I disregarded your pain and made you show up for the ones you knew would habitually abuse you.

I am ashamed that I let them torture you and keep you a prisoner in lackluster love.

I am sorry I never tucked you in at night and told you how proud I am of you, and how utterly strong you are.

I am sorry for the weeds I let infiltrate your chambers.

I am sorry for being a negligent caretaker.

I am so sorry. Can you ever forgive me?

Happiness

When you're having a great moment and joy is singing in your veins, you will regress for a second, *and you will think of him*. Why does he show up when you're so happy, you ask?

Because *happiness attracts happiness*, and at one time *he was the reason for your happiness*. You will think of his smile and the way you melted when it was intended for you. You will remember the words "I love you," and they will buckle your knees.

But know it is a momentary roadblock on your highway to healing. You're stronger now, and you *can go on* without so much as a stagger. You will focus on the happiness you currently feel, and you can push the memory of him to the back of your mind. But it's still there. *It will always be there.*

You're just much stronger now, and you can carry it without it weighing you down.

She Let Go

She had to let go, not just of what she held in her heart, but of what she carried in her mind *every second of every day.*

Shark-infested Waters

Once I put my angst in writing

and share my journey of swimming

in shark-infested waters of heartbreak,

I promise to take your hand,

and show you that fear

is frightened

by resilience.

Journals of Heartbreak

How do we catalogue our pain

and have it at arm's length

for easy reference?

Do we keep our dog-eared notebook

of past loves close to our heart

so we can recall every detail

of betrayal?

Or do we bind the experiences into

the lining of our soul so we can

never forget?

Choices

She often wonders why she chose the way she
did. Why did she chase after those who made
her prove her worth? Why did she have to
tunnel through debris of the past and walk
across tightropes to find her equilibrium?

Why did she feel like she was fighting for her
life instead of chasing stars and embracing
love under the moonlight?

Suppression

We live in a world that wants you to forget and be silent.

It equates strength with suppression.

But in order to heal, you need to let your feelings *feel*.

You need to let your heart release anything that crowds its walls and causes it discomfort.

Don't let pain walk in your home and squat, rent free.

Feel its intensity, then let it go.

Staying Strong

When you acknowledge pain, you validate its impact on your life.

There will be those who will try to disregard your hurt or downplay its intensity.

Try as you may, you will never be able to make them understand how it *affected you*.

How it severed your confidence.

How it reshaped your thinking.

How you spiraled downward into someone you couldn't recognize anymore.

They will not understand how those hands held and hurt you until you were immobile and helpless to reach out.

They wrongly believe that anxiety and depression are self-inflicted.

Separation

You have to separate your hurt from your hope.

And if you can do that, you can move forward.

Voice of Reason

Does the voice of reason

ever listen to its own voice?

In her case: *no*.

Honey, I'm Home

When dark thoughts come banging at your
door, don't bolt it.

You can't expect every visitor in your life
to be beaming with joy and happiness.

Stop believing in coincidences and start
seeing each encounter as a life lesson.

None of us want pain in our lives, but would we
appreciate happiness without having felt it?

Trying Again

One day your heart will be ready to try again.

You will decide this when you realize that living alone with a heart full of love hurts worse than the fate of taking another chance.

You're not naïve anymore.

Skin Deep

You never know

what lies beneath the skin.

A smile can hide

enormous hurt.

Some people

just wear pain well.

Irrelevant Opinions

There is a time to stand up for what you believe in, and a time to *let them believe what they want.*

Learn which battles will bring you peace.

Staying True to Yourself

She isn't weak *because she feels.*

She is strong because she insists on feeling even though the paralysis wants to welcome her home.

Heart Worth Gold

They both weighed their stake in the
relationship and the difference was:
her heart was nonnegotiable.

Those Voices

Listen to those voices.

The ones that whisper: *You can do anything you set your mind to.*

It's the fear of failure that stops us from pursuing our dreams. Fear has a powerful voice and, oftentimes, we obey its command.

But *those voices*, those hushed tones that breathe with featherlike softness across your ribcage, *those voices*—listen to them.

Smitten

Are you smitten

with the ghosts

that keep you company

in the haze?

Are their hands softer

than the iron grip

that daylight

pulls you through?

Daytime and nighttime

are wayward lovers

who have erected

boundaries for themselves.

However, they still meet

twice a day like clockwork.

Fierce opposites who respect

the other enough to

accept them as they are.

Growing from the Inside

Always respect yourself enough to not let your actions be controlled by the words of others.

Whether they are malicious or affectionate words, your motivation needs to grow from the passion fields of your soul.

Shade

You cannot change

the heat of the sun.

Your only option

is to seek shade.

Heart Stylist

She knew her heart needed a new look.

If only it was as easy as hiring a
heart stylist.

VOLCANIC ERUPTIONS

THROW DIAMONDS UP

FROM THE EARTH'S DEPTHS.

ERUPTION

Survival

I will not apologize for the feelings

I carry as survival upon my back.

My self-awareness was not found

in a book or bequeathed to me

at birth.

I had to unearth it among fields

of heartbreak trails.

Row after row

of forget-me-nots and daisies

that always refused to answer.

Forgetting Her

He told her he would

forget her not,

but forget her *he did.*

Housecleaning

And I know it's time

to dust again

when my feet get tangled

in the cobwebs

that have collected around

my self-love.

Asking Forgiveness

I ask for forgiveness

for the words I have spoken

against you.

For the guttural oaths

and the slander

that I thought you deserved.

I beg you to erase the words

from your memory.

I feel the scars

they have caused you

every time you beat

inside my chest.

Wagging Tongues

Know that if they cannot

break you with their hands,

their tongues will wag

forever.

Masterpiece View

My heart has a talent. It is capable of
painting memories that resemble
masterpieces when, in reality, they are
nothing but forgery.

Hungry and Heartful

We can see through them.

We have already convinced

ourselves that we deserve

better, but then the attention

starts to spill,

and we lap it up

like we are starved.

We mistake them

for sustenance

and we even fool

our souls

for a time.

Comfortable
and Complacent

Don't make yourself too comfortable where
you are. Your body may become complacent,
but your soul will be restless.

Garbage Day

Every time his memory made her wistful,

all she had to do was remember how it felt

to be discarded like garbage.

It was an instant spoiler.

The Past Is Past

You know you have gotten over your past
when you can honestly *see* you have not
become your past.

Wistful Soul

There are times she wants to revisit.

Moments she wants to relive.

People she wants to touch again.

She looks back with a wistful soul and she wants to feel everything that she once took for granted.

Emptiness

She has begun to pull the drapes closed at
dusk because the moon likes to highlight the
emptiness that snuggles beside her all night.

A Wolf's Prowl

She had to learn not to let the day control her.

She had to learn to manage the minutes of the day. It gave her an immense amount of self-appreciation when she recounted morning to night and saw everything she had accomplished.

A determined woman who is not deterred by sporadic behavior from others *moves forward with a wolf's prowl.* Hunting for the life that she has always been denied.

Never an Ownership

Always remember that a relationship is two people in a partnership.

It should never be an *owner*ship.

She Needed a Fix

He would work to

lower her self-esteem

and then build her back up

with his attention.

He made sure

she needed a fix.

Wallflowers

She is unlike the wallflowers of your past.

The blooms who stood in your darkness and refused to grow for fear they would overshadow you. Their roots could never delve deep for fear they would strangle yours.

She won't grow low, circling the trees as decoration, staying within your well-manicured border.

She knows how to sew tragedy into triumph, and she will flourish in spite of the vines of adversity.

Compromising

She compromised with her heart.

She told it that missing

the feeling of being in love

was more acceptable

than missing someone

who fell out of love.

Skin

We were branded.
Initials blazing in
each other's hearts.
But with time,
even scars grow dull
and find a home
in your skin.

Dusky Gray

She is neither a daytime

nor a nighttime

kind of girl.

She feels most alive at

dusk,

when the light

is absorbed by the

dark,

and they blend seamlessly,

making gray.

Changing the Ending

Would you go back

and change the circumstances

that led to the end,

or change the person

who decided to end it?

Universe

If you seek the Universe at night

and soak in all its wisdom,

you will find that stars

are twinkling messengers

for the hopeful heart.

Stardust sprinkled across

a midnight sky

has a way of reminding you

that magic absolutely exists

somewhere in that endless vision.

Look closely.

Skies are seldom silent.

They speak by movement.

Shooting stars will encourage you

to take a leap of faith,

breathe long and hopeful gulps,

and ask you to give your wishes

a voice.

Visiting the Old

She is in the habit of revisiting the *old*.

The *once was*.

The way *she* remembers it.

And maybe recollection is a bit untrustworthy, because her heart gives him attributes he surely never possessed.

Circle Sabotage

The discovery is always worse

than the initial destruction.

Finding out that someone took

advantage of your heart

is a hurt not easily

mended.

Regretful Moments

There are regrets that materialize

when you are at your weakest,

when your mind is unable

to stop them from being

fed to your heart.

Earning Strength

She didn't go to a store

and purchase strength,

but she paid for it

nonetheless

with every painful

experience

she endured

to acquire it.

Internal Eruption

There is always the calm before the storm.

The quiet, the bleakness

before the crashing

of the light.

She quivers in thoughts,

shakes with memories

that vibrate her core

and shock her heart.

Each jolt reminds her:

She flows.

She feels.

Her body reenergizes.

Her vessel recharges.

She feels nothing and then everything

at once. She tells herself that she is numb,

but her soul tells her otherwise.

Hot to Cold

Her memory of him

would jar

and beckon

and scold.

Harsh and heavy.

Running from hot

to cold.

Ants

They attack when your defenses are down.

They try to break you, little by little,

so you will fall to your knees.

They can't handle you at full height.

They think they are imaginative

with their creative ambush attacks.

But they are nothing you have not

encountered before.

They are ants under your feet.

Nature's Metaphor

She skates around their smirks.

She wears storm clouds on her shoulders,

lightning licking her tongue.

But if you look closely,

you'll see the rain falls softly

in her eyes.

Digging

All of her past mistakes

make her want to take

her shovel out

and dig down deep.

Unearth everything

she has tried to bury.

She needs to declutter,

and remove the past for good.

Empty Hunger

When the depression hits, she goes days
without eating. Standing in line at a grocery
store would mean being reminded that her
body needs things to keep it alive.

And there are days when she withholds food
because she thinks she deserves emptiness to
go along with her heart.

But she is rational enough to know that she
also does it to get control over her life. *It
is the one thing that she is in charge of.*

Merry-Go-Round

How do you stop

the world

from spinning

round

and round

like a merry-go-round?

You can't jump off

because the world

owns you,

body and soul.

Manifestation

At some point,

everything you allowed

yourself to absorb

will manifest

in some way.

There is no hiding

from what you

willingly took in.

Flip the Switch

How do we turn a bad day into a great one?

We flip the switch.

We look beneath our hoods.

We replace our soul's fluids.

We top them off with affirmations.

A little tune-up and some overdue self-care
every once in a while will keep your heart
and soul running longer.

Warning Bells

How many times

have those warning bells

gone off inside your head,

and you muffled them

and moved forward

anyway?

Beginning of Beauty

Maybe her strength

and endurance

are where

her beauty

began.

Buried No More

You are precious.

Unearthed from a darkened

hell and salvaged.

You are irreplaceable.

You wear diamonds

around your neck

because you like to

remind yourself

that beautiful things

are created from pressure

in the right environment.

You are buried no more.

Neglectful Thriving

Everything grows as the
days progress.

Some need watering,

some thrive with neglect.

Silence.

Tempers.

Weeds.

Patience.

Resentment.

Promises.

Living One Life

It is never a mistake to follow your dream
or passion in life.

Do not listen to the ones who say get
a real job.

You have one life.

You were not born into this one life to live
how others expect you to.

You are unique, and the unusual qualities,
hopes, and dreams you have *are yours*
and yours alone.

Live your life. Not someone else's.

Feeling Low

How hopeless do you feel

when you find comfort

at rock bottom?

Some are able to make

peace with it.

They never forget the feeling

of the rocks buried

in their backs

as they are forced to live low.

Because low feels like home.

Shedding Season

We crack.

We peel.

Exposing our rawness

and our vulnerability.

We cover our ears from the grumbling.

We stop saying "I can't" to ourselves.

We reserve those words for the people who

try to place obstacles in our paths.

We peel.

We crack.

We grow.

Walking Magic

I see the sparkle

in your eyes.

The moons free of tears

on smiling cheeks.

You are walking magic

tonight,

and your charisma

is inspiring

and enviable.

Thoroughbred

I always see potential

in the downtrodden.

Their pain calls to me

and my heart moves

before I can corral it.

It gallops away,

always a long ride,

and I never know

when it's coming home.

I am a thoroughbred

with a soul that races

and a heart

meant for saving others.

Adversaries

It's true that a woman who has fought
to *let go* has battled the most
difficult of adversaries.

Moonlight Penmanship

And her heart still writes letters under the moon to the ones that promised her forever.

Maybe a part of her hopes that magic will bring them back momentarily,

like a falling star.

Freedom Glows

Under twinkling stars
and moonlight kisses,
she glows with the promise
of freedom.
She has acquired this by never
giving up and by discarding
the expectations of others.
She wears the best version
of herself when she is weightless
under a haunting moon.

Secret Strength

All the secrets that line her spine have bonded together and made her ramrod straight.

Her posture is fortified by everything she has overcome and no longer talks about. It is the secret to her strength.

Transformation

That pain...

That pain will either have you on your
knees for life—begging for help
and understanding—or it can be used as a
stepping stool to reach higher than you
ever imagined you could.

Untouchable

When you can look in the mirror

and say to yourself

that *nothing scares you*,

then you have arrived.

Magician

He was an escape artist.

The magical kind

that penetrates your heart

and leaves just as mysteriously,

with nary a trace.

Caution

We need to remember that there will always be results and ramifications for the actions we take.

One decision, good or bad, can cause a chess game to be played for years.

And our moves seldom play out the way we envision they would.

Impasse

There's still a part of her that aches when she feels the impasse that they both refused to cross.

Palate

You cannot fret over everything.

Life should

not be rejected

by our palate.

It should be savored

in our bellies.

Unique

You are indescribably unique.

Have you ever selected an attribute about yourself that you like?

Do you realize how fortunate you are to possess this?

No one else has your combination
of hopes and dreams
residing in their heart.

No one else is you.

Personal Space

Does your lifestyle encourage toxicity?

Have you carved out an entry for the interlopers invading your boundaries?

Every time we allow them passage, we contaminate our personal space.

It's important that we keep our perimeters free of the weeds that will take over our landscape. We need room to thrive, to grow, to expand.

Seeking Advice

She has learned the hard way
to seek inspiration only from those
who have gotten lost in the same
darkness as herself.

LEFT TO HARDEN,

HER HEART ERUPTED,

BIRTHING DIAMONDS.

AND THEIR BRILLIANCE

WAS UNPARALLELED.

BRILLIANCE

Your Story

You can become inspired by
someone else's story. You can hear it
and it will strike a chord that sings
soprano in the choirs of your soul.

Every note will flood your body with
memory harmony.

But never forget that your story is no
less impactful.

Your story could never be written
or told by anyone as authentically
as you could tell it.

Counterfeiters

What is it that you want to hear?

That you can cover scars, and no one will know? You can do that. That is an absolute. Many do this every day. But they are not living an authentic life. Their souls are always on the run, fearing they will be caught as counterfeiters.

I'm not saying we need to wear our painful pasts on our sleeves for all to see, but don't deny them *their right to breathe.*

Heart Recall

We need to separate the person from
the memory.

The person left, but the memory of them
has not.

And the difficult part about that is it fools
our hearts into believing they have stuck
around because they still care.

Being Aware

You will learn to recognize a pain that is similar to yours when you see it in others. You are empathetic to a fault, so you will see signs before the average person does. You will not be able to erase others' torment or ease their burdens.

But you can offer a hand and a heart that has experienced it all. You can listen and give them a chance to release some of it. Sometimes knowing that someone else has felt it allows the pain to flow out instead of circling back in.

Solarium

She feels forgotten

in the shadows,

but her soul shines too brightly

to be invisible.

Her inner solarium

is surrounded by shattered windows.

On good days

she is sweeping up

and throwing away

a past that is landfills high.

She feels weak,

but she knows it takes strength

to rise and sift through

the shards every day.

There are rare moments

when she bends low, below

the broken panes,

and she can envision a kaleidoscope

reflecting broken things.

Her heart refracts like a prism,

and for a moment she can feel

the incandescent light source

of the universe illuminate

and rejuvenate her senses.

Discovery

She made a discovery when she

pulled the bandages away.

She found out that she was

the same person.

A little beat up inside,

but so much more experienced.

Her eyes are wide open.

Her pain tolerance level is

through the roof.

But those scars?

They do not change her core.

Her soul.

Her essence.

She is still herself.

She made a discovery.

Feel Your Way

I am not hard to understand.

Just listen to the words I do not say.

Nighttime Sounds

Why is the weight of love unbearable
at night?

Is it because there is no light to buffer
the sound of your heart screaming in
the darkness?

Proposal

She hasn't forgotten the way the diamond
captured the moonlight on the night he
slipped it on her finger.

Fear of the Unknown

It's hard to move on when you're
traveling through the unknown.

Your view is so wrapped up in looking back
that you can't see the adventure before you.
All you see is fear.

Constant Companion

She thought that if she worked hard
and stayed busy from sunup to sundown,
she could eradicate him from her day.

She thought the painful images would recede,
but they kept rolling.

And her mind, an avid watcher, kept scrolling.

Don't Tell Him

Don't tell him you saw me like this.

Don't tell him I stopped living

when he said goodbye.

I could not handle his pity again.

Don't tell him I hit bottom

without him there to catch me.

Tell him the person he hurt

does not exist anymore.

Tell him you saw me *smiling*.

He always loved my smile.

Intruder

Somedays,

there is no escaping

fear.

It grips

your throat

and dares you

to breathe.

Self-Awareness

She always sought inspiration from others.

But one day, she realized that *she* was
inspiring herself with her accomplishments.

Lessons

Why do we accept

whichever love *finds us first?*

Maybe because it teaches us

the kind of love we do not need.

Getting Lost

Exploration is never more instrumental in a life than when you choose to explore *another person*. Take the time to get to know someone on the inside.

Don't worry about *getting lost* or finding your way. Lost can be an incredible adventure when you find yourself wandering through another's soul.

Staying Power

The only way

they will see

your *staying power*

and know that you

are *not* an option

is if you *stop*

being one.

Driver

Don't let them steer your way.

It is no longer in their power

to control your journey.

When they become a roadblock,

take a detour.

Go another way.

Never look back

at anyone who would want

to keep you from pursuing

your passions.

Rejection

If we think about it in a positive way, and turn our broken hearts upside down, *rejection is simply being redirected* to another path.

A path that you are meant to walk with your head held high.

The Universe knows where you are meant to be, and it's not a place where you feel rejected.

Wicked Ones

The wicked ones

don't stop being wicked

even after they see

you down.

They just wait

until you rise again.

But know this:

Each time you get up,

you prove you are

stronger than anything

they cast your way.

Undercurrent

She is calm as water

with nary a ripple on the surface.

But she carries with her an undercurrent

that tangles her feet

and loosens her tongue.

Abyss

When she started searching

for a way out of the abyss,

she wandered through caverns

of disrespect dripping with denial.

She dug her way out,

and what she unearthed

was a chest full of diamonds

more valuable than

anyone else's approval.

Interpretation

We hold on to the one percent chance

that we are going to make

their hearts sing a song

that only we can interpret.

Snap

I am wound with years of remorse,

and I am learning how to twirl

and release the knot,

slowly,

so I don't snap.

Seeking Gold

If she paints her world

in hues of rainbows,

will her heart be inspired

to travel

and seek the pot of gold

at the end?

Refusal

Goodbyes are hard

when a heart refuses to wave

or say goodbye

at the door.

Hourglass

If each grain of sand in an hourglass represents a moment in time that she can never replace, then her hourglass will never stop flowing.

Come In

Her heart is wide open.

Her doors are pulled wide,

hanging off their hinges.

Her welcome mat is perfectly placed

and ready to call them in.

She stands on her stoop

and breathes in sunshine.

She is ready to love again.

Inner Fist

She has promised herself that she will not
allow the past to taint her future.

She will no longer envision how her life
might have been, but will instead create the
life she should have.

She will knock the memories back with her
inner fist instead of drowning them in
Friday night sympathy cocktails.

Questions Under Moonlight

She was curious and she wondered countless
things. Even her soul could not keep up with
the list of questions.

It could not tell her *why* some flowers
thrived, and others withered.

Why the sun and the moon kept their distance
from one another.

Why the moon highlights a soul's desires and
the sun distracts the heart.

Or *why* some people *fall out of love.*

Pressure

When you are under pressure, you will feel
overwhelmed, even suffocated, by what is
expected of you.

You reach deep down and you try to give
more. You empty yourself until you are a
walking shell.

You do this because you are a giver,
but it can only go on for so long.

Remember to *give to yourself,* too.

Instruction

If you want to teach someone something,
it is best to instruct by performing the
task *with them*.

Only speak from experience.

Never try to tell someone else how to live if
you have never ventured into their world.

Never tell someone else how to love if you
have failed miserably.

Never give advice on a subject if you have
only read about it, but never lived it.

Railcars of Strength

Some view her as weak because her body
fights this world daily.

But they only see her diagnosis.

Her nemesis is invisible, but she still
shows up with her motor running.

She has railcars of strength
riding up and down her spine,
and she moves them daily on tracks that
she lays by hand, one by one.

She never knows what tomorrow holds,
but she is grateful for every day that she
has a chance to move.

Gift Giving

If you have come to terms with your past
struggles, you can share what made
them transpire.

Sharing your past is a gift.

Choose your recipients wisely.

It is a sacred offering you give to another.

You can share your pain and it can be full
of wisdom.

But remember, you don't get a say in how they
use your personal story.

Endings Foretell

The endings of relationships display

how someone handles

pain,

rejection,

and

finality.

Falling

There are times I fall.

I unlock the floodgates.

I allow it all to come back.

I resurrect every memory I buried.

They carry me away with the force of a
hurricane, and I feel weightless as I return
to a place where I no longer belong.

There are times I fall.

I allow myself this self-torture on occasion
as a reminder that I am not there anymore.

I am not stuck there.

I know my way back.

I let myself feel the pain and the shame,

and then I get up

and lock the floodgates once more.

Foolish

She feels foolish

when she thinks about

the amount of time

and the amount of love

that she stored in his care.

She was always the one

who tried to make sense

out of situations

that made no sense.

Calming Light

With every experience

you grow,

until one day

your soul emits a light

that provides a calming warmth

and blankets your fears

so you can continue your journey.

People Pleaser

You know they laugh at you when your back is turned, and it causes that lump in your throat and that knife in your chest.

But have you asked yourself why their opinions and their approval mean so much to you?

You worry about your looks, and your job, and your home. But what about the contents of your soul?

Are you giving your passions and talents an honest and authentic review?

If you care more about what they think of you than what you think of yourself, you're not.

Peeking Out

When the memory of him rolls in
with sirens blazing, I peek out
the curtains of my soul and watch
his approach.

He looks the same way he did
the last time I saw him.
Arrogant.
Unsettled.
Lost.

I close the curtains back
and remind myself that I *now*
have the strength to stop viewing life
through the windows
of the past.

Stepstool

I will never bow down

to anyone who wants

to use me as a

stepstool.

Cloud Watching

The sky changes colors and the clouds stand at attention as she tells them of her struggles.

She vents openly,

the heavens her audience.

She watches the clouds move like acrobats.

They toss and turn, roll back and forth, restless and unable to handle the words she shouts.

She screams obscenities meant for no ears but her own, and the birds go silent.

The sky turns dark

and the clouds roar angry.

But still, they have no answers for her questions.

Actions Prevail

Communication is good, but it cannot replace actions.

You cannot talk your way through life without ever lifting your hands to work.

Triumphs

If we documented every struggle
we endured during the day,
our calendars would be filled with triumphs
instead of white space.

Heavy Goodbye

When we parted,
the cinders turned to ashes
and the winds blew them away.
And I wanted to ask the clouds
to carry them back, but they
could not contain the weight
of the love being thrown away.

No Halves

I will not share.

I don't want love in halves.

I deserve its entirety.

Sunday Best

She has taken this life

and worn it

like her Sunday best,

hiding her weekday duds beneath.

Measuring Stick

How easily can you walk away?

That is usually a good ruler to measure the intensity of the connection.

The Beginning

Meet me back at the beginning.

Where the stars lined up and parted the skies, drawing a line from me to you.

Meet me in the space.

Where we reached inside the darkness, touched hearts, and found each other.

Meet me under the trees.

Where we lay, spending countless hours retelling our pasts in grand detail.

Meet me under the arch.

Where we professed our love and promised for better or for worse.

Meet me at worse.

Where we chose to ignore the promises and the trees as we navigated the dark void of stars.

Nature Is Poetry

I smell flowers.

I watch the trees billow.

I feel the sky cry.

Nature has a way

of speaking poetry

without saying a word.

Wasted Days

There was a time when the days were long.

The minutes were an eternity.

They would drag on,
and all she wanted was for them to be over.

The calendar blared empty,
showcasing all the days she was wasting.

She wanted time to stop controlling her soul,
so she set the calendar on fire.

And she had no regrets as she watched the
paper curl up and burn away.

I Believe in You

I believe in you.

In your testimony of strength

and your song

of redemption.

Diamonds

She's been through more hell than you'll
ever know.

But that's what gives her beauty an edge.

You can't touch a woman who can wear pain
like the grandest of diamonds around
her neck.

Acknowledgments

To Kevin, my children, my mom, and my grandchildren, who have had to endure my hermit status. Thank you for loving me. *I love you.*

Regina, I will always love you for believing in me and for your gentle nudge.

Ashley, Gypsy, Amy, Rula, Angie, Melody, Kevin, Courtney, Jeannine, Tiff, Lynette, Stephanie, Madalyn, Liz, Nicole, and Cheryl. Your unwavering friendship and *belief in me* are the reasons I continue to write. *I love you all.*

To Jesus Christ. You are the reason in every season of my life. Thank you for taking me on the pathway that has led me to today.

A big thank you to my readers. This is for you!